The **WIMP'S GUIDE TO**

The **Supernatural**

rated by
e Smith

by
Tracey Turner

**First published in 2013
by Franklin Watts**

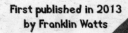

Text © Tracey Turner 2013
Illustrations by Dave Smith
© Franklin Watts 2013
Cover design by Cathryn Gilbert
Layout by Jonathan Hair

Franklin Watts
338 Euston Road
London NW1 3BH

Franklin Watts Australia
Level 17/207 Kent Street
Sydney, NSW 2000

A CIP catalogue record for this book
is available from the British Library.

ISBN: 978 1 4451 1459 0

1 3 5 7 9 10 8 6 4 2

Printed in Great Britain

**Franklin Watts is
a division of Hachette
Children's Books, an
Hachette UK company.**

www.hachette.co.uk

CONTENTS

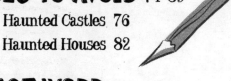

INTRODUCTION

There's nothing wrong with being a wimp. It makes perfect sense to be scared when, for example, **a grey lady glides through your bedroom wall.** There's a wimp inside all of us, and he or she is there for a very good reason.

The supernatural is anything that doesn't obey the laws of nature — unexplained stuff — like **dead people wandering about with their heads under their arms.**
In fact, there's a surprising variety of supernatural phenomena. . .

- **GHOSTLY APPARITIONS**
- **MYSTERIOUS BEASTS**

- PEOPLE CHANGING INTO HAIRY KILLERS DURING A FULL MOON

- HOUSEHOLD OBJECTS HURTLING THROUGH THE AIR ON THEIR OWN

. . .to name just a few. Prepare yourself, because we're about to meet some of them.

WWWWhhhhoooooooo
WWWWhhhhoooooooo

WWWWWbhhhooooo

Hang on, what was that? Did you hear something just then? A sort of eerie moaning, and a clanking sound? Maybe it was just air stuck in the pipes, or the wind. **Parp!** Anyway, let's not worry about it. It was probably nothing.

So, now you're ready...

BANG

Nyar har har har har!
Nyar har har har har!

. . .it's time to stare scary stuff straight in its evil, bloodshot eye. Read on to discover the horrifying details about the supernatural. Most importantly, learn the best way to get away from whatever's giving you the heebie-jeebies as fast as you possibly can. . . by harnessing the power of your inner wimp.

BANG
BANG

Um. . . You don't think this book could be haunted, do you?

GHASTLY GHOSTS

Ghosts are the spirits of dead people. Sometimes they appear, other times they just chuck stuff around. Just thinking about it sends a shudder down the spine of any jelly-belly wimp.

wooooooo

While there's no hard evidence that ghosts exist at all, the people who believe they've had encounters with ghosts seem very convinced.

WAAAAH

Mists, Orbs and Shadows

OOOoo! Pretty...

According to witnesses, ghosts can appear as **glowing balls of light** that hang in the air, or sometimes zoom about. Other ghosts appear as mysterious shadows and swirling mists — like smoke, or even mini-tornadoes.

Glowing balls of light seen near marshes are sometimes known as **will-o'-the-wisps**. One explanation is that the lights are **evil spirits** trying to lure travellers away from safe paths and towards dangerous places, such as cliff edges. Another explanation is that the lights are caused by **swamp gases**.

As for mysterious shadows and swirling mists — hmmm. Could they be, in fact, shadows and mists? Sometimes no one knows anything about them until they see them in a photograph.

Pah! Even us wimps aren't frightened of that. The chances are, it's just a speck of dust caught by the camera flash, or a hair or something. And, even if you actually see a **Sinister Shadow of Death** or **Mysterious Ghostly Orb** right in front of you, surely it's not as frightening as watching someone walking through a wall. Speaking of which. . .

Apparitions

Wimp Rating: 8 out of 10

Grey ladies, blue boys, phantom coaches, people carrying their own heads . . . there are records of ghostly encounters like this, and others. Imagine yourself in the following ghastly situation. . .

A WIMP'S WORST NIGHTMARE

You whimper to yourself. Why did you agree to spend midnight at a ruined castle on the edge of Dartmoor in Devon? It's deathly quiet . . .

apart from a thudding noise. It's growing louder and louder, coming across the moor. **Gaaaaa!** Four ghostly galloping horses are thundering towards you pulling a coach! A black dog with glowing red eyes is running along next to it. You scream as you realise the coach is made from bones! There are human skulls on each corner at the top, and the driver has no head! **This is ... just wrong.** You hide in the shadows and cover your eyes. You know you shouldn't, but you take a peek. **Aaarrrggh!** There's a ghost woman inside the coach, and she doesn't have any eyes!

Phew! That was close. According to legend, you've just seen the ghost of Lady Howard. She lived at Okehampton Castle in the 17th century.

HACK

Every night at midnight she rides to the castle in her coach made from the bones of her four dead husbands. Once there her fiendish hound plucks a blade of grass, which he takes back to Lady Howard's old home near Tavistock. She is doomed to make the journey until every blade of grass at the castle has been cut. **Hasn't she heard of a lawnmower?**

AT ASHEVILLE HIGH SCHOOL IN NORTH CAROLINA, USA, A GHOSTLY APPARITION APPEARED...

A) EATING LUNCH IN THE CANTEEN

B) IN THE STAFFROOM

C) ON A CCTV CAMERA

D) IN THE TOILETS

Answer: C). In the middle of an August night in 2008, motion sensors started a security camera, which filmed a dark shape moving across a corridor. At one point it seems to form into the shape of a child.

There are plenty of reports of apparitions. For example, Blickling Hall in Norfolk was the childhood home of Anne Boleyn, second wife of Henry VIII, who had her head chopped off.

Henry! I lost my head over you!

On 19 May, the anniversary of her execution, Anne Boleyn is said to arrive at Blickling Hall in a phantom coach. It's driven by a headless coachman and pulled by four headless horses. Anne Boleyn gets out and carries her own head around the house until dawn.

Anne's father, who betrayed both Anne and her brother to try to save himself, also haunts the house on the anniversary of his death. He races around the grounds driving a coach, pursued by howling demons (which must annoy the neighbours). The legend says that he will continue to appear until a thousand years have passed since his death, which won't be until 2539.

If that's not scary enough for you, there are more terrifying stories of haunted houses on page 82.

TERRIFYING TRUE TALES

THE HIDEOUS FACE

A writer called Dennis Wheatley had a
horrifying childhood experience at his
boarding school in Kent in 1910. As he was
climbing the stairs to bed he saw a hideous,
white, bloated face on the other
side of the banister. It was just a few
centimetres from his own face. Dennis
screamed and the figure ran up the
stairs. The school was searched, but
no one was found.

Later, Dennis discovered that teachers at
his school held séances (meetings to try to

communicate with the dead). They believed that the horrible figure was an evil spirit they had summoned that evening. Dennis said that seeing the hideous face was the most terrifying experience of his whole life.

Poltergeists

Instead of showing themselves as shadowy or ghostly figures, poltergeists make their presence felt in other ways. They chuck things around, and bang and crash about the place. They are the most annoying ghosts on record!

HAUNTED BED

One poltergeist made a nuisance of itself in Savannah, Georgia, USA, in the 1990s. Things started happening after an antique bed was brought in the house: objects were moved and thrown, photographs overturned and — spookiest of all — the young boy sleeping in the bed felt cold breath when he lay in it! The poltergeist wrote notes to the family, revealing himself as a seven-year-old boy called Danny, who didn't want anyone sleeping in the bed because — **look away now if you're easily scared** — his mother had died in it. **Eeeek!**

"GEF", THOUGHT TO BE A TYPE OF POLTERGEIST, HAUNTED THE IRVING FAMILY ON THE ISLE OF MAN IN THE 1930S. HOW DID IT MANIFEST ITSELF?
A) AS A TALKING TEAPOT
B) AS A TALKING MONGOOSE
C) AS A TALKING HAMSTER

Answer: B). Gef claimed to have been born in New Delhi, India, in 1852. Only two people outside the Irving family actually saw Gef, but several said they'd heard his voice.

RECTORY POLTERGEIST

Borley Rectory in Suffolk was supposed to be the **world's most haunted house** until it burned down in the 1930s. It was haunted by a poltergeist (as well as a nun, a girl in white and various headless men).

The pesky poltergeist would:

- lock people inside rooms
- throw bottles and other objects
- write ghostly messages on walls
- make loud noises in empty rooms

However, after the fire, the woman who lived at Borley said her husband was responsible for the "poltergeist" activity — making him the most annoying husband on record!

HAUNTED OFFICE

At Rosenheim in Germany in the 1960s, two scientists from the Max Planck Institute were called to an office to investigate poltergeist activity. This included rotating pictures on walls, moving filing cabinets, and malfunctioning photocopiers, lights and phones. All the activity happened when a particular office worker was present, but the scientists couldn't prove she was responsible.

Weird Ghosts

Dead people hanging out in the land of the living is weird enough. But some ghosts are especially weird. . .

THE HAIRY HANDS

On the B3212 road, in Dartmoor, Devon, a pair of hairy hands occasionally makes an appearance. You might think there's nothing very spooky about that, but the hairy hands aren't attached to a hairy person! A caravan owner spotted them on her window, and a motorcyclist claimed that the hands tried to force his motorbike off the road.

Wimp Rating: 8 out of 10

ANIMAL GHOSTS

It seems that dogs and cats are frequent visitors from the afterlife. For example, a headless black

Wimp Rating: 6 out of 10

dog haunts the area around Avening in Gloucestershire, giving people a fright by brushing up against them. Thankfully, it can't bite, for obvious reasons.

GRRR. . .

Stories of ghostly black dogs have been told for centuries — seeing one is supposed to mean that you will soon die.

The **phouka** is an Irish spirit that takes the form of a ghostly horse and carries victims off on wild night-time rides. **Yee-ha!**

BELIEVE IT OR NOT. . .
The Snarly Yow is a black dog that
haunts western Maryland, USA.
Several drivers have spotted it in
the middle of Route 40 and thought
they'd run it over. When they stop to
investigate, they can't find anything.

Screaming Skulls

There are various accounts of skulls that don't like to be moved. If they are, there are terrible consequences: objects are

thrown about and hideous screams ring out. The most famous skull is kept at Bettiscombe Manor in Dorset. It is supposedly the skull of an African slave whose dying wish was to be buried in his homeland. The skull seems to have made do with Dorset though, because it screams and causes disturbances if anyone tries to move it.

! FACTS WIMPS NEED TO KNOW !

WHAT TO DO IN A GHOSTLY ENCOUNTER

◊ Don't panic! After all, it's only a spirit returned to Earth from the dead . . . er . . . OK, **panic!** But remember that not all ghosts want to frighten you.

◊ Don't creep about in the dark — turn on the lights! Carry a torch with you in case of power failure. Ghosts are far less likely to appear in well-lit areas.

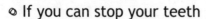

◊ If you can stop your teeth chattering, say something in a stern voice, such as **"Please leave this place immediately!"** Some ghosts are — apparently — very obedient.

◎ This may sound obvious, but don't go anywhere that's supposed to be haunted on your own (duh!). Ghosts seem to like individuals, and are more likely to appear. Some turn nasty when they spot someone on their own. The headless ghost at Scarborough Castle tries to drive lone visitors over the battlements to their deaths. Stick to your friends like glue!

◎ Finally, remember that ghosts were people once. Be polite and considerate of their feelings. Then back away and run like mad.

So terribly sorry . . .
but I must dash. . .

THE UNDEAD

The undead are a group of creepy creatures that were dead, but have come back to life. The undead are also called the living dead. With the right tools and preparation, you'll be ready — to run away really fast. . .

Zombies: The Living Dead

Zombies are the living dead of your nightmares (and countless horror movies). They are dead people who have been reanimated by supernatural power. They can often be seen staggering about with hideous gaping wounds, their arms outstretched, moaning away. **Oh, and they feed on living flesh!** Just in case you're not sure how to identify one of them, here's a handy Wimp's spotter guide. . .

FACTS WIMPS NEED TO KNOW

HOW TO SPOT A ZOMBIE

- Unhealthy-looking, greyish skin
- Bloody wounds — which may look fatal
- Missing limbs
- Blank stare
- Arms held out in front of body
- Staggering gait, dragging feet
- Lack of conversational skills
- Groaning/moaning
- Smell of rotting flesh

If you can say "yes" to two or more of the boxes, it's almost certainly a zombie. What are you waiting for? **Run!**

ZOMBIES AT THE MOVIES

A film called *White Zombie*, in which a young woman is turned into a zombie using a voodoo potion, was the first ever zombie movie.

It was first shown in 1932, and since then hundreds more zombie films have been made.

You can also encounter popular versions of the living dead in computer games such as the classic "Zombies Ate My Neighbours", in which you have to defeat the evil Dr Tongue, who shoots tongues at attackers. Urgh!

WHICH OF THE FOLLOWING ARE REAL TITLES OF ZOMBIE FILMS?
A) LET SLEEPING CORPSES LIE
B) *THE INCREDIBLY STRANGE CREATURES WHO STOPPED LIVING AND BECAME MIXED-UP ZOMBIES*
C) ZOMBIES! ZOMBIES! ZOMBIES!
D) PRIDE AND PREJUDICE AND ZOMBIES

Answer: All of them are real zombie film titles. (Yes, even *The Incredibly Strange Creatures Who Stopped Living and Became Mixed-Up Zombies*.)

HOW TO ESCAPE A ZOMBIE ATTACK

○ **Avoid the zombie bite.** A zombie on its own is only a small threat. The real problem is that zombies bite and infect other people, creating a dangerous zombie army.

○ **Use your speed.** This is your best defence, since zombies shuffle along slowly. However, they are very determined. Keep running until they're far away (or because someone else has bashed them — see opposite).

⊙ Scatter obstacles behind you as you run.
This will slow down zombies. Locked doors present a particular problem to the living dead because they lack the brainpower to look for keys. They could, of course, just smash down the door.

⊙ Don't try to talk to a zombie — it will not be distracted and will probably only groan horribly in response.

⊙ A blow to the head is the only way to stop a zombie. Since they cannot feel pain, sustained head-bashing may be required.

Real Zombies

Wimp Rating:
8 out of 10

Those are the kind of zombies you might see in horror movies. But – **try not to squeal in terror** – the movie zombies are based on *real life*. People who practise the voodoo religion, popular in Haiti and parts of the southern United States, believe that zombies really do exist. Voodoo priests, they believe, have the power to reanimate dead bodies and set them to work as slaves.

40

What's brown and sticky?*

BELIEVE IT OR NOT. . .

Baron Samedi is a powerful voodoo spirit, and it's his job to make sure dead bodies behave themselves and don't return to walk the Earth as zombies. He has a skull face, wears a top hat, smokes a cigar, drinks rum and tells rude jokes. Sound like anyone you know?

*Answer to joke: A stick.

TERRIFYING TRUE TALES

THE ZOMBIE SLAVE

In 1962 in Haiti, a man called Clairvius Narcisse was declared dead. His family went to his funeral. Eighteen years later, a man claiming to be Clairvius Narcisse appeared in his hometown, and was recognised by his family.

His horrifying story was that he had been turned into a zombie by his own brother, who made him work as a slave. He claimed that he had escaped two years later, but remained in hiding from his brother for many years, and only came to find his family again after his brother died.

Could Clairvius Narcisse really have been
turned into a zombie? Wilfred Doricent
is another person who was, apparently,
zombified. In 1988, aged 17, he became ill
and **"died"**, and was buried in a tomb. Days
later, he turned up in the middle of his village
— alive, but unable to speak. Some people
believed that Wilfred had been made into
a zombie by a voodoo priest.

ZOMBIE POWDER

A possible explanation is that Wilfred Doricent and Clairvius Narcisse (and there are other cases too) really did become zombies — but not because of supernatural powers. Perhaps they were given a **zombie poison** to make them appear dead, as some ex-voodoo priests have suggested. The recipe for the poisonous zombie powder contains:

◦ **Tetrodoxin** — a powerful poison found inside puffer fish. It can paralyse a human being so that the person appears to be dead, but is in fact aware of everything around them. Too much can kill a person though.

⊚ **Datura** — a poisonous plant that can cause confusion and loss of memory if it's eaten.

I'm not really here. Ribbit.

⊚ **Cane toad toxins** — poison found on the skin of cane toads can make victims see things that aren't really there.

Whichever explanation you prefer — supernatural zombies or zombie poison — it's totally terrifying.

Blood-sucking Vampires

Wimp Rating: 8 out of 10

A WIMP'S WORST NIGHTMARE

It's a hot summer's night, so you leave the window open when you go to bed. The curtains billow in the breeze. You lie in the darkness for a while, wondering about the weird stories you've heard lately about mysterious fanged strangers, but finally you nod off. You have a dream in which you see a cloaked figure crouching on the window behind the curtains. It jumps on top of you and holds you down. He opens his mouth to reveal . . . hideous fangs! **Aaarrggh!**

You wake up in a cold sweat and sit bolt upright — but no one's there. It was just a nightmare. Hang on, though . . . there's something warm and sticky on your neck. You go to the mirror to have a look. **Gaaaaa!** There are two puncture wounds on the side of your neck. . .

Aaarrrggghhh!

Actually, it's all right. It really was just a nightmare. Just take deep breaths.

Vampires, like zombies, are another example of the undead. During the day they rest in their coffins. Then at night they rise up and go in search of blood to feast on. If that wasn't bad enough, often the vampires' victims become vampires themselves, and go off in search of yet more victims. **Good grief!**

Deadly Dracula

There are legends about blood-sucking vampires all over the world, and some of them have been around for thousands of years. The most famous vampire story is Bram Stoker's *Dracula*. It's about a mysterious count in a region of Romania called Transylvania, who turns out to be a vampire, and a group of vampire-hunters who are on a mission to destroy him. It's not recommended for those of a nervous disposition. The writer took Count Dracula's name from a real Romanian

ruler, Vlad Dracula, who was also known as Vlad the Impaler because of his nasty habit of impaling his enemies on wooden stakes.

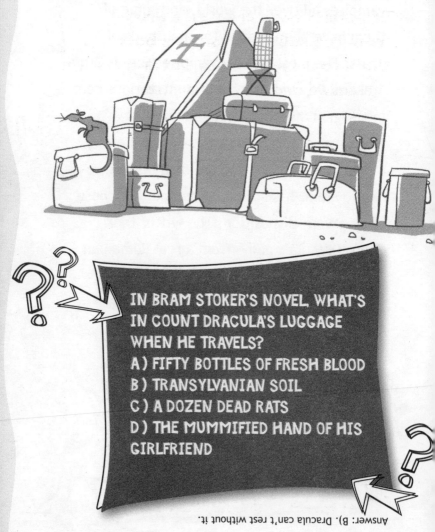

IN BRAM STOKER'S NOVEL, WHAT'S
IN COUNT DRACULA'S LUGGAGE
WHEN HE TRAVELS?
A) FIFTY BOTTLES OF FRESH BLOOD
B) TRANSYLVANIAN SOIL
C) A DOZEN DEAD RATS
D) THE MUMMIFIED HAND OF HIS
GIRLFRIEND

Answer: B). Dracula can't rest without it.

BELIEVE IT OR NOT...

Scientists have created a drug from the saliva of vampire bats that stops blood from clotting. It's called Draculin, after the famous blood-sucking count.

WORLDWIDE VAMPIRES

The fanged, blood-sucking vampires from Transylvania — wearing a swirling black cape or long white nightdress, and with traces of blood around their mouths — are just one of the different types of vampire from around the world. . .

○ In China, vampires have green or pink hair and red eyes.

○ Greek vampires are half-woman, half-winged snake.

◇ In Malaysia, the blood-sucking Penanggalan is a flying head.

◇ An Aboriginal Australian yarama-yha-who is a small red creature that hangs from trees and sucks the blood of passers-by using suckers on its hands and feet.

Keep an eye out on your travels.

Vampire-Hunters

In the past, many people in Europe really did believe in vampires. From the Middle Ages until the nineteenth century, real vampire-hunters dug up corpses suspected of being vampires, and performed gruesome rituals to prevent them from rising from the grave.

I thought you brought the ladder!

TERRIFYING TRUE TALES

THE SERBIAN VAMPIRE

In 1725, a Serbian farmer called Peter Plogojowitz died. A few days after his burial, Peter was spotted in the village where he had lived. Within a week or so, nine people from Peter's village had died in mysterious circumstances . . . and before they died, they claimed Peter Plogojowitz had attacked them.

The villagers opened Peter's coffin to discover that his body had not decomposed, his hair and nails had grown, and there was fresh blood in his mouth. The villagers were in no doubt that Peter was a vampire! The villagers took a wooden stake and drove it through his heart — supposed to be the only way of killing a vampire. Then they burned the body for good measure. Oddly, the mysterious deaths stopped.

IN THE UNITED STATES, AND CENTRAL AND SOUTH AMERICA, THE BLOOD-SUCKING MONSTER THE CHUPACABRAS IS SUPPOSED TO FEAST ON THE BLOOD OF...
A) CHILDREN
B) DOGS
C) GUINEA PIGS
D) GOATS

Answer: D) The name Chupacabras means "goat-sucker" in Spanish. The creature is supposed to feed on goats and other livestock. Sightings say that it has fangs, spines and glowing red eyes, but the real culprits could be sickly dogs or coyotes.

In the late nineteenth century, around the time that *Dracula* was written, people in Rhode Island in the United States believed that some victims of a lung disease called tuberculosis became vampires. They thought the dead rose from their graves at night to suck the blood of their relatives, dooming them to die from the same disease. To stop the "vampires", the bodies were dug up and the hearts removed and burned.

FACTS WIMPS NEED TO KNOW

HOW TO THWART A VAMPIRE

If you're ever confronted by a vampire, it shouldn't be that hard to frighten it off. Vampires are scared of lots of things — in fact they're probably even more of a wimp than you are. They're afraid of:

◊ **Garlic** — just as garlic is a natural repellent to nasty, biting insects such as mosquitoes, it also repels nasty, biting vampires.

◊ **Sunlight** — vampires shrivel and die in the light and can only come out under cover of darkness.

○ **Crosses** — especially crucifixes, but even your crossed fingers will make them shudder.

○ **Mirrors** — in which, spookily, vampires have no reflection.

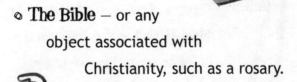

○ **The Bible** — or any object associated with Christianity, such as a rosary.

○ **Wooden objects** — especially stakes — can be used to kill vampires. Metal weapons won't work.

Any of the above should be enough to keep vampires at bay.

LYCANTHROPES

It's not a pretty word, is it? L-Y-C-A-N-T-H-R-O-P-E. These supernatural beasties aren't pretty either. They transform into dog mode under the light of a full moon. Maybe they were cursed. Maybe you shouldn't hang around to find out. . .

Hairy, Scary Werewolves

Werewolves are human beings who transform into a wolf — or half-wolf, half-human — when the moon is full. They return to their human form when dawn breaks. Some werewolves are just born that way, while others gain the power to transform into a wolf using magic potions, chants or objects.

Maybe I should brush my face, too.

LEGEND SAYS YOU'RE LIKELY
TO BECOME A WEREWOLF IF:
A) YOU'VE GOT GREY EYES
B) YOUR BIRTHDAY IS ON
CHRISTMAS DAY
C) YOU'RE THE SEVENTH SON
OF A SEVENTH SON
D) YOU'RE ALLERGIC TO TOMATOES

Answer: B) and C). Although there aren't
many seventh sons of seventh sons about,
plenty of people are born on Christmas
Day, so you'd better watch out.

Stories say that if a werewolf bites or scratches
another person, the victim becomes a werewolf.
Real wolves are scary enough, but werewolves
are even stronger and more ferocious and
bloodthirsty — they'll eat anything that moves,
and quite a lot that doesn't.

A WIMP'S WORST NIGHTMARE

You decide to walk home across the moor one evening by yourself. After all, what's the worst that could happen? It's cold, windy and dark, and you stumble along the path, struggling to see until a full moon comes out from behind the clouds to light your way. That's better . . . but what was that strange shape in the darkness? You start to run.

OOOooooooWWW!

A terrible howl rings out — the howl of a wolf. You run faster, but you can hear the sound of something galloping along behind you. **Oh no!** You feel hot breath on your back. . .

SILVER BULLETS

If you are ever confronted by a werewolf, silver bullets are supposed to be the only way of killing it. (Some say you can use any silver weapon.)

Unfortunately, the silver bullet will need to be fired from a gun — and there is a lot of evidence to suggest that guns are much more dangerous than werewolves. According to some accounts, the Beast of Gévaudan (see page 70) was killed using a silver bullet.

Real Werewolves

During the 1500s and 1600s, France was Werewolf Central. Tens of thousands of werewolf sightings were reported around the country. During the period from 1520 to 1630 there were an average of five reported werewolf sightings per week!

I'm having a howling good time!

French people must have been scared witless. If the reports were true, a huge number of people must have been growing hair and fangs, and going on the rampage every full moon.

BELIEVE IT OR NOT. . .

Some people still believe that crimes and traffic accidents are more likely to happen during a full moon, and in 2007, British police departments even added extra officers at the full moon to cope with the expected mayhem. But there's no evidence to suggest that it's true.

WEREWOLF CRIME

Criminals were often accused of being werewolves, or claimed to be werewolves themselves, and sometimes they were executed as werewolves. . .

○ **Pierre Burgot and Michel Verdun** were put on trial in Poligny, France, in 1521. They confessed to various murders, and said they transformed into werewolves using a magical cream.

◦ **The wolfman of Padua** in Italy was convinced he was a wolf (a mental illness called lycanthropy) and attacked and killed people in 1541.

◦ In Germany in the 1580s, **Stubbe Peeter** was a farmer who confessed to killing and eating people and animals while transformed into a werewolf. **Gross!** He said that he was given a magic belt by the Devil that allowed him to change into a wolf when he wore it, and to change back again when he took it off.

THE BEAST OF GÉVAUDAN

In the 1760s, wolf-like creatures killed dozens of people in central France. Witnesses said the beast (or beasts, as it turned out) was reddish in colour, with a long tail and huge teeth. Some reports even said the beast walked upright on its two hind legs. Many people suspected a werewolf was on the loose.

PROFESSIONAL WOLF HUNTERS

The King of France sent professional wolf hunters to find the man-eater, which seemed to prefer to prey on people rather than animals. In 1765 a big male wolf was shot, stuffed and put on display at Versailles. But, much to everyone's horror, the attacks continued. Finally, a local hunter shot and killed a second beast and the attacks finally stopped.

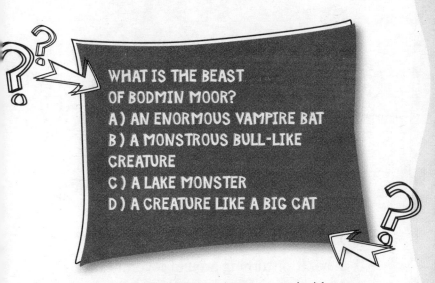

WHAT IS THE BEAST
OF BODMIN MOOR?
A) AN ENORMOUS VAMPIRE BAT
B) A MONSTROUS BULL-LIKE CREATURE
C) A LAKE MONSTER
D) A CREATURE LIKE A BIG CAT

Answer: D). According to various reports, the Beast of Bodmin Moor is a big cat. Similar reports turn up every so often in different parts of England. But they haven't killed any people . . . at least, not as far as we know.

WEREWOLVES: TEN TELLTALE SIGNS

Do you suspect someone of being a werewolf? Look the following checklist. Does the person have:

1. Excessive hair, especially on hands, and eyebrows that meet in the middle?

2. Long, dirty fingernails?

3. A habit of turning around several times before lying down?

4. Meaty breath?

5. A large and indiscriminate appetite?

6. Superhuman hearing?

7. A tendency to whine, snarl or howl?

8. An adverse effect on people with pet allergies?

9. A habit of bolting their food?

10. A record of being found sleeping outdoors the morning after a full moon?

If you answered "yes" to one or more of the questions — especially if one of them was question number 10 — the person may well be a werewolf. Stay away from them at full moon, and avoid sleepovers.

PLACES TO AVOID

Some places are just perfect for supernatural critters to set up residence. Perhaps a terrible event occurred on the site, or in the building. Either way, you'd better hope it's not on your paper round!

Haunted Castles

It's no surprise that there are countless stories of haunted castles. They're dark, ruined, centuries-old places, with dank dungeons where all sorts of unspeakable things have happened.

Here are two you probably won't want to visit:

CHILLINGHAM CASTLE

Wimp Rating: 7 out of 10

The appropriately named Chillingham Castle in Northumberland is home to a whole host of ghosts.

The most famous ghost is the **Blue Boy**. Just before midnight, a visitor staying in the Pink Room in Chillingham Castle would hear the terrible screams of a child. As the cries faded and the clock struck midnight, a bright glow in the fireplace would form itself into the shape of a young boy dressed in blue.

In the 1920s, part of the wall in the Pink Room was demolished and . . . the skeletons of a boy and a man were discovered! They were buried, and since then the Blue Boy hasn't appeared, though blue flashes sometimes flicker along the wall in the dead of night.

Other ghosts at Chillingham include:

◎ The ghost of **Lady Mary Berkeley**, who makes herself known by the rustle of her dress, and an icy cold blast of air.

◎ A ghostly woman who steps out of a painting in the nursery.

◎ Whispering voices in the library, which stop as soon as anyone tries to listen to what they're saying.

⊙ A white lady who haunts the pantry in the basement.

⊙ Outside, an entire ghostly funeral procession which appears in the garden.

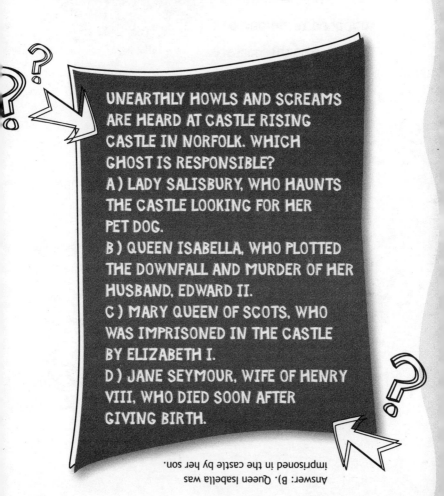

UNEARTHLY HOWLS AND SCREAMS ARE HEARD AT CASTLE RISING CASTLE IN NORFOLK. WHICH GHOST IS RESPONSIBLE?
A) LADY SALISBURY, WHO HAUNTS THE CASTLE LOOKING FOR HER PET DOG.
B) QUEEN ISABELLA, WHO PLOTTED THE DOWNFALL AND MURDER OF HER HUSBAND, EDWARD II.
C) MARY QUEEN OF SCOTS, WHO WAS IMPRISONED IN THE CASTLE BY ELIZABETH I.
D) JANE SEYMOUR, WIFE OF HENRY VIII, WHO DIED SOON AFTER GIVING BIRTH.

Answer: B). Queen Isabella was imprisoned in the castle by her son.

Glamis Castle

Make a mental note: never visit Glamis Castle in Scotland. It's supposed to be one of the most haunted places in the whole world. Here are just some of its many ghosts:

◊ A ghostly woman with a bleeding mouth. Some say she's a vampire (there's a story that the family who lived here had one vampire in each generation), others say that she was a maid whose tongue was cut out to stop her from talking about a crime she witnessed.
Yikes!

◎ The ghost of Earl Beardie gambles with the Devil for eternity in one of the castle rooms.

◎ King Malcolm II of Scotland — he died here and some say he was murdered.

Best of three?

◎ A butler hanged himself in a room now known as Hangman's Chamber, and his ghost haunts the room.

◎ The ghost of an imprisoned boy haunts the Mad Earl's Walk on the castle ramparts.

◎ A monster — or the vampires mentioned opposite, whichever you prefer — are locked up in a secret castle room.

◎ The Grey Lady haunts the chapel — she is thought to be the ghost of Lady Janet Douglas, who was burned as a witch in the sixteenth century.

Haunted Houses

Unless you're a king or queen, or a billionaire or something, you're very unlikely to live in a castle. But lots of us live in houses. Hopefully your house isn't one of these:

MONTE CRISTO

Wimp Rating: 6 out of 10

The Monte Cristo homestead, a Victorian manor in Junee, New South Wales, is supposed to be Australia's most haunted house.

It's haunted by the ghosts of Mr Crawley and Mrs Crawley, the original owners (Mrs Crawley gets quite stroppy and sometimes orders people out of the dining room).

A ghostly woman also appears on the balcony, thought to be a maid who fell to her death.

HOW DOES THE GHOST OF QUEEN VICTORIA MAKE ITSELF KNOWN IN THE BEDROOM OF HER ISLE OF WIGHT HOME, OSBORNE HOUSE?
A) SHE REARRANGES THE FURNITURE
B) HER GHOST SLEEPS IN THE BED, AND DISAPPEARS IF ANYONE APPROACHES
C) HER FAVOURITE PERFUME, ORANGE AND JASMINE, SOMETIMES WAFTS AROUND THE ROOM
D) SHE WRITES MESSAGES ON A NOTEPAD BY THE BED

Answer: C). Visitors sometimes catch a phantom queenly whiff.

The Whaley House

Wimp Rating: 7 out of 10

The Whaley House in San Diego, California, USA, was built by Thomas Whaley in the 1850s.

It was built on the site of a gallows, and one of the ghosts that haunts the house is Yankee Jim Robinson, who was hanged there in 1852. Thomas Whaley and other members of the Whaley family all put in ghostly appearances from time to time, along with other ghosts, including a ghostly girl who sometimes grabs people by the arm, and a ghost dog who licks visitors' bare legs.

The Baleroy House

The Baleroy House in Philadelphia, USA, was built in 1911. Some of the many visitors who come to see its antiques have reported all sorts of ghostly apparitions.

A WIMP'S WORST NIGHTMARE

You're visiting Baleroy House, wandering around the upstairs rooms, when you hear shuffling and tapping downstairs. When you look, there's an old woman in the hallway tapping on the floor with her cane — but she seems to glide. It's suddenly very cold. You turn and almost walk into a monk in a brown habit. There's something very weird going

on here, because he's gliding too. You start to panic, and rush downstairs to the ground floor.

In the Blue Room, a blue mist hangs in the air. You remember a ghost story you heard yesterday — that the Blue Room is haunted by an evil spirit known as Spectral Amelia, who appears as a blue mist.

Aarrgh! You feel a bit faint and collapse in a chair. A curator rushes in and pulls you up. "Don't sit there!" he says. "That chair is supposed to be cursed. Don't worry, though, it's only if you sit there in the presence of Spectral Amelia that you'll die." **Whew! That was close!**

Don't sit there!

FACTS WIMPS NEED TO KNOW

HOW TO TELL IF YOUR HOUSE IS HAUNTED

Use these helpful questions to find out:

1. Are there unexplained cold spots or draughts in the house?

2. Are you ever approached by ghost-hunters who want to spend the night in your house?

3. Are there unexplained odours in the house? *

4. Do you ever feel you are being watched when there's no one else in the room?

5. If you have portraits on the walls of your house, do the eyes of the subjects seem to follow you?

6. Do you ever hear voices or other noises coming from rooms you know to be empty?

Crreeaaakkkk!

7. Do you ever see transparent people vanishing and reappearing through closed doors and walls?

8. Does your dog or cat ever seem agitated for no obvious reason?

If you said "yes" to more than two of the above, especially if one of them was number 8, your house could well be haunted.

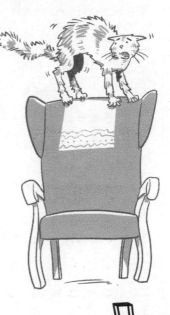

* It could be a ghostly whiff, like Queen Victoria's perfume on page 84. **Phewee!**

Last Word

You've been very brave. You've come face to face with headless ghosts, a haunted photocopier and a talking mongoose. Now, you're armed with vital information on how to identify werewolves, outwit zombies and evade vampires and ghosts.

But you might have noticed something from this book: although there are plenty of reports of supernatural phenomena, there's not really any **evidence**. And, as far as we know, no one's ever been actually harmed by a ghost. There are plenty of far more scary things for a wimp to worry about. . .

. . .SPIDER!

Your Wimp Rating

Answer these questions with **"yes"** or **"no"**. How many do you answer **"yes"** to? Add up the number to generate your very own wimp rating on page 93 — go on, how tough are you **really**?

Wimp Rating: ?? out of 10

1. It's Hallowe'en and your friends want to dress up as zombies and go out in the dark. You say. . .

2. You're with a friend at Scarborough Castle when they need to go to the loo. Do you stay on your own?

3. You're offered a place on a school visit to the Whaley House. You say. . .

4. You're taking a walk out in the woods, when a strange glowing light appears. Do you go over and investigate it?

5. You hear a howling noise and scratching at your door late at night. Do you open it to see what's going on?

6. You win free tickets to see Blue Boy at Chillingham Castle. Do you go?

7. You'd be happy to go on a school exchange trip to Asheville High School, North Carolina, USA.

8. You're on holiday in Scotland, visiting Glamis Castle. Are you first in the queue to get in?

9. A friend hands you a wooden stake and invites you on a vampire hunt. You say. . .

10. You'd be happy to stay with an auntie who hates garlic and stays inside during the day.

How many questions did you answer "yes" to?

Three questions: you're a novice wimp – not quite chicken enough yet.

Four questions: you're a wannabe wimp – you don't scare easily.

Five questions: you're no fraidy cat – more like a werewolf.

Six questions: you laugh in the face of fear.

Seven questions: you've got guts – all hanging out like a zombie's.

One question: you're a mega wimp — your favourite food is cowardly custard.

Two questions: a champion wimp — you wouldn't say boo to a goose.

Zero questions: you're the Ultimate Wimp — well done! You have truly given your inner wimp a great big hug.

WIMP-O-METER

Eight questions: you'd be happy sleeping in a haunted horror house.

Nine questions: you're not afraid of any ghosts or ghouls or spirits.

Ten questions: oh, dear! You're not even the least bit wimp-like — but you are slightly bonkers! Reach out and embrace your inner wimp.

Glossary

Aboriginal here, of the people who first lived in Australia

Afterlife the life believed to follow death

Crucifix a model of a cross with a figure of Jesus on it

Dartmoor an area of wild, high ground in Devon, UK

Decompose to rot

Eternity time without end

Gait the way someone walks

Habit here, the long item of clothing worn by medieval monks

Impale to pierce with a sharp stick

Indiscriminate done without making a careful choice

Legend an old story handed down from the past

Maid a female servant who did much of the housework

Middle Ages the period of history from around 1000 to 1450

Monk/Nun a member of a religious community

Pantry a small room near the kitchen used for storing food or cooking equipment

Prey on hunt for food

Puncture wound a deep cut

Reanimate bring back to life

Repellent something that helps to keep something away

Rituals special ways of doing things in a ceremony

Rosary a string of beads used by Roman Catholics for keeping count of prayers

Stake a strong post, sharpened at one end

Supernatural phenomena things that cannot be easily explained

Index

The WiMP'S GUIDE TO

illustrated by Dave Smith

JUNGLE SURVIVAL

by Tracey Turner

EDGE

978 1 4451 1461 3 pb   978 1 4451 1465 1 eBook

Have you ever:

Paddled down the Amazon River? ✕
Been stung by a scorpion? ✕
Gone without food for a day? ✕

**If you answered NO to all of the above
then this is the book for you!**

Terrified of bugs? Great! Feel sick about
travelling? Fantastic! Inside you can read
about loads of crazy stuff and how
to survive – or avoid it.

Love your inner wimp!